# Retails from the Crypt

(You know… it's the title of the book you bought?
Or stole. Or borrowed. Or "borrowed.")

## By Matt Square

ISBN: 978-0-578-56740-2

Cover design by Argama Witch

## "Praise" from random people who haven't read *Retails from the Crypt*

"I've read some books. Boy howdy have I ever read some books, but this is the one I liked." — Woody Battaglia of Almost Tuesday on WAY 104.3 FM

"No. And you can quote me on that." — Christopher Lee Van

"No." — Ashley Smith (That's her real name. I didn't just use a generic name generator.)

"This is a book that was written by Matt. It has multiple words and pages. Utterly readable in English." — Kate Ciavara

"Well... it's a book." — Jen Pendergast

"One time Matt wrote a book. Here it is." — Mike Peterson

"I have been assured that this book exists." — Bob Killingman

"I've read a lot of books in my life, and I'm not quite sure if this was one of them." — Melissa Willard

"This is 20 pages of material spread to 50 pages. Truly an inspiration to high school English students across the nation!" — Shaun Papineau

"It appears to be a novel." — Chris Carty

You will finish reading this book, having read a book. Truly a piece of writing set to the page." — Collin Henderson

"It uses words and punctuation to achieve the goal of imparting an idea to the reader, assuming they are both literate and speak the same language." —Bob Klingerman

"What kind of book?!" — Kate Ciavarra (again)

"Another one?" — Nathanial Karahalis

"Blurbs about what? I don't understand." — Nick DeStefano

"What kind of blurbs?" — Sarah Dauplaise

"What's your book?" — Samm Brush

"I expected to be disappointed. I was disappointed." — Andy Carlson

"I miss your cat ears." Caitlin Martinez

"I uuuhhhhh...didn't read it" — Ryan Sears

"I want to speak to this book's manager." — Dane Sager

"Item arrived quickly and in perfect condition. A flawless transaction!" — Sarah Dauplaise (again)

# Contents

# The Case of the Mysterious Disappearing iPods

I wanted to start this book out with a bang, so here is the story of several missing iPods. I also want to quickly mention that I'm a very sarcastic person who very rarely takes anything seriously. That being said...

It was the autumn of 2005 when I was 18 and had entered my first job in retail. I worked at an electronics store, and I could not have been more excited. Not only did I have a fascination with new technology, but I was also a very avid photographer. It seemed to make sense that I ended up in the digital imaging section of the store. It would only be a matter of time before I learned the horrors of retail and how they consume your soul. I would soon become jaded and learn a lesson that I would carry with me from job to job; the management in retail (actually, most jobs in general) tends to be incompetent and will have a negative impact on everything.

Every morning at the store started with a rigid routine. The employees would come in an hour before the store opened and ready their respective departments. Then, 10 minutes before open, we would all come together and have a short meeting to discuss various issues and goals. I quickly noticed there was one topic that was discussed frequently — the fact that we always seemed to be missing iPods. No matter how many times they would adjust the inventory to factor for the shortage, we found it wouldn't take long before the count was off again. Management would stick to the idea that this was due to external theft. They were always quick to blame the employees and our "carelessness," often throwing out the phrase, "We need to be vigilant!"

Corporate tracked theft statistics at the store level and gave each store sort of an "allowance" of how much product was expected to be stolen in a given year. If a store was able to prevent such theft, then the store would get to keep that extra money as a bonus to split among the employees. Not only were we told by management to be vigilant against shoplifting, we were also constantly asked, "Don't you want your bonus? I know I do!" just to make sure there was this sense of guilt or loss to add to our apparent negligence.

The employees, including myself, had their own theories about this alleged "shoplifting." It wasn't exactly impossible for a customer to steal an iPod, but it was unlikely, as they were kept in a locked case. So short of an employee accidentally leaving the case open or someone kicking in the glass, the problem didn't seem to be shoplifters — at least in the high numbers which the iPods were missing. The employees had come to the conclusion that this was an inside job, but management didn't believe us (and what would we know about anything anyway?). We were clearly peons to our management overlords. What value could our ideas be to management of such intellectual expertise? Why should they listen to anything we had to say at all? How could they even hear us? Who better than Kanyon? Also, where?

A couple of months into my employment, management had worked out a plan concerning the iPods. Instead of keeping the iPods on the sales floor where they were susceptible to thievery, they would place all of the iPods locked in a cage on top of an aisle. This was a foolproof plan because, in order to take an iPod, you would have to climb a giant ladder in plain view to get it. This plan was so solid that it took the entirety of TWO full weeks for our inventory count to be off again. We were told to be vigilant and be on the lookout for shoplifters because they clearly not only had master lock-picking skills but also invisibility cloaks.

Many of you readers may have wondered something at this point: how could the employees be so sure that iPods weren't all *actually* being stolen by shoplifters, as management suggested? There is an easy explanation for this. After the suspended cage plan didn't pan out, management had moved the cage to a more secure spot. It was moved into the Loss Prevention room —a room for which only managers and Loss Prevention employees have a

5

key. Furthermore, in the Loss Prevention room, the iPods were in a cage that only managers had the keys to. This was it! This was the master plan! How could any iPods go missing with this kind of complex security? They couldn't! Well... except for the 50 or so iPods that went missing after that. "Keep vigilant!"

So what can be deduced from all of this information? On the surface, it would appear that none of literature's greatest detectives: Holmes, Poirot, Marlowe, Columbo — or even Batman — could solve this daunting mystery. In all seriousness, despite the fact that I am not Batman, I think I've worked out a theory. If you are reading this, and I assume that you are, you're probably also not the world's greatest comic book hero either, but we are probably on the same page about what happened to these iPods. It was ghosts. Clearly. What else would you expect me to say in a book called Retails from the Crypt? It's obvious the answer should be spooky, and what's more spooky then the dead coming back to utilize modern technology? AND it's not like management would be stealing them. They live on a higher moral plane than the rest of us. I'd go so far as to say being retail management is just below being knighted by the queen herself and slightly above being an Olympic medalist. There is no way that it could have been the manager who happened to put a down payment on his house that was roughly, but suspiciously, close to the value of 50 stolen iPods. It probably had nothing to do with his manager friend either. A friend that was fired from another company for throwing pallets of merchandise into a trash compactor. Why would those two managers have ANYTHING to do with merchandise going missing?

Look, I don't want to name names or mention what store it was, mostly for legal reasons. I'm also not accusing anyone of stealing iPods or that the stories I mentioned about those managers are even true, again, mainly so I don't get sued. I'm just saying, that we clearly have a ghost issue and should have called the Ghostbusters. Oh, and we should have been "vigilant." You can't spell vigilant without ghost.

Actually, my spellcheck is indicating that I'm wrong, but whatever.

# A Child's Murder is Announced

Those in management aren't the only people who are trying to ruin your work day. Coworkers can often be the very reason you stay at a job for longer than you expect. They often become good friends. But, there is usually also at least one coworker who can make your job harder than it needs to be, or is awkward, or a big creep.

I have a great example of this, but I want to mention right now that I am a very paranoid person. I'm the kind of person who — while everyone is being nice to my face — thinks they're secretly talking behind my back and planning my demise.

I worked on the planogram team at a department store and had a coworker on the team who I'll call Lester. (Planogams are just blueprints of the stores aisles and where all the products are supposed to go. They change all the time so our job was to take an aisle down and reset everything.) Lester seemed like a pretty normal guy in his early twenties. He talked a lot about his daughter, who was around 5 at the time. You could tell how much he loved her just by the way he talked about her.

Lester and the mother of his child had broken up by the time he started working with us. The mother had a new boyfriend and also had custody of the child, but Lester still got to have time with their daughter. It seemed like the relationship between all the parties involved was quite amicable, and there weren't any problems.

One day, Lester had taken a phone call and then told our manager that he had to leave immediately and was very panicked. The next day he called and told us there was an incident with his daughter. The mother and her boyfriend had gotten into a fight and things had gotten physical. At some point, the daughter was knocked down the stairs and had to be taken to the hospital.

There were even more complications at the hospital. The daughter was given an anesthetic that she was allergic to. This would end up doing damage to her lungs. A few days later, Lester came into work to give us an update. His daughter's lungs were in bad shape, and she would need a lung transplant soon. Unfortunately, lung transplants for 5-year-olds are fairly hard to come by, but Lester kept his hopes up.

The next week was kind of awkward. Lester took a week off but would often come in for a couple hours and play video game demos on the stores kiosks. Like I said before, I'm pretty paranoid so I thought it was kind of weird that he was doing that, but my other coworkers assured me it was probably to get his mind off things.

Amazingly, after about a week of waiting, the hospital called Lester and said they were able to find a match, and the lungs were being transported over from another state at the moment. It was nothing short of a miracle — they'd have the lungs by that night and would be able to operate the next day.

The planogram team and the other employees of the store waited to hear what happened the next day. Lester called to us what happened, but it wasn't the news we were expecting. The lungs were too late.

His daughter had died the night the transplant had arrived. The funeral and wake were scheduled, and information was posted for any employees who wanted to attend and support Lester. The store had done the usual and sent flowers to the hospital and later to the funeral home, and a card was passed around for everyone to sign and send condolences.

The whole planogram team, being the closest to Lester, went to the wake. I was the only one on the team that decided not to go. I wasn't that close to him, and I thought he was kind of annoying. He immediately started working again after the wake.

It made things especially awkward for me because I really felt like I was walking around eggshells around him. Sometimes I can blurt out things randomly without putting much thought into it, which can often be offensive (nothing too offensive, but it was obviously a very emotional state and I didn't want to bother him in any way). And then there was my paranoia, which was telling me that something about Lester and this whole situation was kind of sketchy. I admitted all of this to a coworker of mine who was also a friend of mine and he responded, "Wait, did your planogram team not tell you anything?"

It had turned out that the wake the planogram team went to never actually happened. They went, but no one was there save for Lester, who greeted them and told them the funeral home had cancelled the wake and locked down the building with his daughter inside. As the team drove back home, my manager called the funeral home and asked them if there were any services planned recently under the daughter's name and they confirmed that there was not. She had also contacted the police to see if there was a police report filed on the date that the daughter fell down the stairs and again the answer was no. Even when the store had sent flowers to the hospital, they were sent back with a note saying there was no one there by that name.

The next few months working with Lester were quite strange. We didn't know if his daughter actually existed or not, but we were sure if she did, he was clearly lying about her death. It would have been illegal for the store to ask for proof of the death. No one was sure if we should call him out on that because clearly, he was insane, and we didn't want him to murder us or something of that nature. He wouldn't shy away from mentioning his dead daughter after the fact, maintaining that the funeral home had her body indefinitely.

It was interesting to know that my suspicions about Lester and his story were right, but it wasn't reassuring to know I was working with a psychopath. It's not what I'd call a win-win situation. After all that information came out though, my paranoia did kick in a couple more times. The story was so crazy that sometimes I felt like everyone was lying to me as some kind of joke or weird social experiment. That or, fitting in with the theme of the book, I would come in one day and ask, "Where's Lester? I haven't seen him in a while."

A coworker would turn to me with a confused look and ask who I was talking about. I would explain and they would just respond with, "No one by that name works here, what are you talking about?"

I would then walk away and suddenly notice a newspaper clipping taped to the wall amongst other papers. The article would describe a man named Lester who died of heartbreak on that very day 600 years ago, on that very spot after his daughter died in a tragic accident. Truly horrifying.

One more thing before I bring this story to a close. I was talking to someone on the team whom I will call Dave. Dave needed some money to pay some bills that came early, and so he asked Lester if he could spare him until they got paid that Friday. Lester agreed. Dave later mentioned to me that when he went to Lester's house to pay him back Lester's mother answered the door. She said she would take the money for him because Lester wasn't there — he was at the playground with his daughter...

# Retails from
# the Crypt (Intro)

You may be thinking to yourself, "Why would you put not the introduction to book at the not beginning of book" and all I have to say to that the sentence structure when you think that to yourself is not great.

If you must know, I thought the iPod story was just more interesting than any introduction I could write, so essentially, this book will somehow get progressively worse as you read on. That's saying a lot because those first two entries weren't that great, but if you made it this far, thanks! Just keep on trucking along. You might as well.

Anyway, I have had over a dozen years of retail experience. I've worked at a party store, a sporting goods store, an electronics store, a grocery store, and a regular department store. That's just retail. I have the "pleasure" to say I've also worked in a cash vault for an armored car company and as a telemarketer. I wouldn't suggest working at any of these places and they are generally jobs you should avoid, but sometimes, it can't be helped. I do think that everyone should be required to work in retail for one year no matter what their background is — as a humbling experience. Maybe that would make customers a little nicer, but probably not.

I decided to write this book for a few different reasons. First, I wanted to address the major problems of working in retail, which I have identified as the "Triumvirate of Dickheads You'll Meet at Work." The triumvirate is composed of customers, managers, and coworkers. Most of the time, the job itself is fine. Not the most exciting, but whatever. It's the people that make work  more frustrating and difficult.

You've read about idiot managers and strange coworkers already, but I saved my favorite, customers, for last. After that, I'll give you a little advice about why these problems exist, some work-life balance tips, bite-size retail stories, and then I'll end the whole thing with some podcast recommendations. You could have just read the contents page to figure that all out — me writing this here adds to the overall length of the book. More importantly, it accomplishes the hidden goal of this book — wasting your time. This paragraph is a fine example of that.

Another reason is that I really want to win a Pulitzer. I don't think I actually will, but it won't happen if I don't try. Actually, I don't really expect anyone to really read this book. When I really think about it though, even if no one reads it while I'm alive, who knows what the future will bring. A lot of artists become hugely popular after their deaths. Maybe this book is amazing, it just before its time.

I like to imagine this book becoming one of the great American novels that is a standard read in high school. Much like how *Catcher in the Rye* can fill a teen with angst and existential feelings of growing up, my book can introduce young adults to the futility of work. Or it be a cultural study of our time in an age where all work is done by robots. OR it could be a cultural study of our time in an age where all work is done by humans for robots who have enslaved humanity.

I want to think that in this theoretical popularity of my book that not only will I win a Pulitzer, but every accolade possible. Future generations will obviously want to see the movie version of this, and so I'll win an Oscar. The TV show that will come shortly after, which will follow the tertiary characters more closely, will ultimately win me an Emmy. I'll be offered a Grammy for the soundtrack for both and speaking of music, did I hear someone say *Retails from the Crypt: The Musical?* Tonys, here I come! The ultimate award would be the Nobel Peace Prize (it can't be given posthumously, but I think they can make an exception for me). Maybe this is a book that will bring peace to humanity.

Of course, there will be the smaller awards too. Whatever garbage prize podcasters get, maybe an MTV award. I think you can see

21

where I'm going with this by now. The possibilities are endless though. If you want to make your life a little better, you can spend some time thinking about it too. Every day, think of one award this book can get.

This isn't the first book I've written. That's the final reason I'm writing this. Don't bother looking up the other one – it's garbage. I see this book as a sort of redemption for a book that I was embarrassed to have written. This may not be the best book in our generation, but I still consider it much better than something I wrote in high school. I'd like to say it would be a good exercise to see the progression through the years from my first book being really bad, my second being kind of bad, and so on, but I'm never writing another thing ever again. Too much work, and it's not worth either of your or my time.

I hope you can find some enjoyment in the book though. My goal is to make you smile at least one and cringe at least 3 times. If you worked in retail as well I hope reading this sets off some of your own memories of horror and trauma that you thought you had hidden away in the deepest parts of your mind.

# The Receiving End
## of it All

Working in retail, you get the chance to meet thousands of different people. Each person can have several traits that differentiates them, giving them their own distinct personalities, much like the many snowflakes that litter the Massachusetts landscape in the winter. But, as you begin to meet more customers, you will learn that there are a lot of larger, more general, traits that link these customers together. You have the "this is too much" customer, who is related to the "I'm shopping somewhere else" customer, and then there is the talks-to-you-way-too-much customer, the customer that thinks you don't deserve any respect because you're working in retail, and so on. Customers are, of course, the last of the... whatever it is I called it before. The

Trifecta of Retail Dickheads? I don't know. That's already one essay ago, and I can't be asked to remember that far back. Anyway, here are the few types of customers you can meet.

Decades ago, it was customary for people to have a bit of privacy in their lives. You would never talk about religion or politics openly, but now with advent of social media, data-stealing websites, and the NSA spying on us, it's hard not to know every intimate detail of a person's life — whether you want to or not. No judgement here — live however you want to live. The more introverted customers tend to harken to the days of yore and at least attempt to keep parts of their lives private. For instance, while I was working in the photo department, I noticed a customer circling the aisle that had our photo kiosk on it. After a while, I approached him and asked if he needed any help. He had told me that he wanted to print a few pictures from the kiosk, but wasn't sure how the process worked, and I agreed to help him. I took his photo card and placed it in the kiosk and began explaining the process. It was then that he turned to me and asked, "Do the pictures on the card show up on the screen? I have some pictures that I would like to be private." My heart sank. I knew immediately the weight of his words and what they had meant. Before I could do anything, the pictures loaded on the screen, and we both turned to look. He pointed to a nude photo of his wife and said sheepishly, "Yeah, that's the picture that I would like not to be seen." He ejected the card on his own and made his way out of the store, his head hanging low.

Unfortunately, this kind of humility is not within all customers. Other customers also have private details of their lives, but it is apparent that this is of no consequence to themselves and they really don't mind who knows any detail of their lives. During my first week of training at one store, I was placing signs in the aisle with men's deodorant. As I was performing this task, a woman came into the aisle and started looking through the several variations of deodorant. After a few minutes of searching, she looked to me and asked which deodorant I preferred, and I told her that I didn't use it. She looked back at the seemingly endless choices she had in front of her, and there was a brief moment of silence. Just when I thought the conversation had ended, she looked back at me and said, "Women's deodorant isn't strong enough for me, so I have to use men's." She could have responded that she was shopping for her husband, she could have said she forgot which brand her son used, she could have said NOTHING at all, but instead, she thought it would be pertinent information for me that she needed this product for herself. Again, no judgement — it's just not really information I needed to know about a random person. It is just a really weird way to meet a person, I guess.

I have another example of customers having a lackadaisical stance on privacy, and it is the way in which they use their cell phones. It would seem that, to these customers, being on the phone is a private affair, regardless of whether they are in public or not. If you ever been in a large retail store, you may have noticed that cell phone reception is dubious at best. To counteract this, some people believe that yelling

into the phone somehow helps. Case in point —
while I was working, I happened to overhear a
woman talking to a friend on her cell phone
when the reception gave way. She started yelling,
"What!? No! I said! No! I said I went to the! I
went! I went to the doctor! The DOCTOR! No,
the doctor! No, he said! He said I! He said I have
a yeast infection! A yeast infection! I HAVE A
YEAST INFECTION!"

As I was listening to this conversation,
three aisles away, I began to wonder what I had
done in a past life to have to deal with this, but
I've found that it's best not to think too hard
about it.

There is also the jokester customer, who
just can't help themselves and has to make the
same joke you've heard a million times. Such
gems include:

- Employee: Do you need anything else?
  Customer: The winning lotto numbers!
- Alternate to the above
  Customer: A million dollars!

- A comment on your unique name that seems interesting to them, but you've had to deal with everyone saying the same exact thing because you've had that name your entire life.
- Singing a song or making a reference to the employee's name.
- Customer: If it doesn't have a price tag (or if it isn't ringing up at the register) it must be free!
- Customer to cashier: I printed that bill recently! Looks good right!
- (Employee brings out a product from the warehouse that the customer asked for) Customer: That's not what wanted! Ah, just kidding!
- Customer: I don't even need to go to lunch, I'll just go around and eat all these free samples!
- Customer: Does it come with this? (Points to a lady, or car, or any kind of desirable object that the product is pictured next to.)

I could go on and on and on and on with this list, but it hurts me to keep thinking about it.

In the many experiences I've had in retail, I've learned that not every customer is out to make your job miserable — just a large majority of them. In all seriousness though, you can meet a lot of interesting people on a daily basis. The only problem is, you get to meet a lot of *interesting* people as well.

Oh yeah, I guess I'm supposed to make this creepy or something to fit with the title. Give me a second to look through my book of horror tropes...ok I got it!

*Oh my god, the customer are coming from within the house! Get out of there!*

# When It's Time to Tardy, We Will Tardy Hard

I'm late. I'm late all the time. I've been fired from a job for showing up late too many times. Quick note though: the store manager didn't care that I was late, there was just one manager who had some kind of grudge against me being late. He waited for the store manager to go on vacation and then called corporate about me to have me fired. There was a specific reason I was always late to that job. They regularly scheduled me to do a closing shift and then an opening shift the next day. Also, they scheduled me to come in an hour before the store opened. That was normal because they wanted employees to set up their departments and make sure they were tidy before the store opened. The flaw in that was the only thing I really needed to do in the camera department to get ready was turn on five display TVs. I made sure the department was neat before I left the night before, so there wouldn't be anything to do in the morning. I figured instead of coming in an hour before the store opened, I would come later. No one really cared except for that one manager, and other people in the department did the same, so I am not sure why he picked me specifically, but whatever.

I would say it's because I'm not a morning person, but really it's just I'm not really a waking up person. It doesn't matter what time of day it is. I'm just too friendly with my snooze button. I've actually missed a shift at work once because I didn't set an alarm. The shift started at 2PM, so I assumed I'd be awake by then, but I ended up sleeping for 24 hours straight. Since I never call out or miss a shift, the managers were concerned and asked me about what happened the next day I came in. It was pretty weird trying to explain that I was asleep the whole time.

This trait has followed me from job to job, and I've had several managers at several different jobs talk to be about being anywhere from 5 to 15 minutes late consistently. I can remember one job in particular that had an issue. The tardy employees were all tracked on the computer, and the store was scored by corporate. I had tried very hard to get on track and to stay on time. One such tactic was that I would set my clock so that it was 15 minutes earlier than the actual time. That worked for a while, but eventually, I thought I was just getting used to it. So I would set it 15 minutes earlier again. It wasn't long before I realized that it was an automatic clock and after a while, it would automatically reset the clock to the correct time.

One year, the store was scored poorly on tardiness, and so management decided to have a contest. If an employee could go without being late or calling out for one specific month, they'd be entered into a raffle to win a big-ticket item. I figured I was already trying to get into the habit of being early anyway, so this was perfect timing for me.

The month started out pretty good. I had a few close calls, but I managed to get into work on time for the first three weeks. Then the day came. I saw the clock and knew it would be tough to make it on time. I'd be late by a minute or two. I got up and rushed out the door, but a third of the way to work I figured it was futile. It became very clear I wasn't going to make it.

Just then, the song "Push It to the Limit" came on the radio, and I got inspired. I thought, "I've come too far to give up this easily." I hit the gas and started speeding to work. Everything started working in my favor, and there were no cops around the spots that they usually were. Every stoplight turned green for me. It was all so serendipitous.

I sped into the parking lot and ran to the time clock. I got there and saw I had less than a minute to punch my number in. Once it registered, the clocked ticked over only seconds later. I had literally made it with seconds to spare. I never felt so exhilarated at that job, but maybe it was because of all the blood rushing to my head from running. It was all thanks to that random song that gave me the courage to fight on. Only one more week of this, and I'd have accomplished a whole month of being on time and on my way to winning a TV.

The very next day, a big storm hit the area and my house, alarm clock and all, lost power, and I was an hour late. That should teach me to ever put any effort into anything ever again. This isn't an essay about the Triplet of Retail Fools either, so I don't have to end it with a horror trope, so I'll just end it abruptly.

# Carl and Chris

I started writing creatively during my leisure time when I was in the 7th grade. Whatever I could think of just manifested itself out of my brain in the form of poetry, short stories, essays, comic books, and screenplays. I am not sure what set off this personal renaissance, but ever since, I have had a remarkably strong passion for writing. I have even written and published a book (on top of this one), a feat that seemingly loses its value over time, as it seems everyone has written one now or, at the very least, had one ghost written in their name. Recently, I was going through my collection of works, and I realized that I have not really grown that much as a writer. Indeed, I can objectively say that most of the works I have written are garbage. It is this fact and my love for writing that make it so difficult to write this essay. The essay needs to be well written in honor of those it will describe and because I am writing it as a personal reminder of the value of my time and life. Frankly, I am pretty sure that I am incapable, but I will do my best.

It was on Monday morning, 3 a.m., when I stumbled onto my bed. I had difficulty sleeping that night. I decided to do some homework until I was sufficiently tired. I guess my plan did not work as well as I had thought because in only an hour or so I would again be awake and staring at my ceiling. That is when I noticed my phone had been vibrating. I remember thinking how weird it was that someone had texted me that early in the morning. Using my powers of rationalization, I concluded that maybe someone from work was calling because an emergency had arisen in the middle of the night.

Nevertheless, it was not an employee's name I saw but my brother's. He sent a message to inform me that my sister's fiancé, Chris Corcoran, at the age of 33, had just suddenly died. There seems to be a Pavlovian response when you find out that someone familiar to you

39

has died at a young age. It can be either a quiet thought to oneself or a loud exclamation, but it is always "What!?"

I know this because that is what I said to myself when I read the text. It is what my girlfriend said when I told her. It is what my girlfriend's mother said when she received the news.

Chris's wake was held on Saturday of that week followed by his funeral on Sunday. I knew I wouldn't be able to keep my composure because even though we had known each other for about two years, we had literally not exchanged more than five sentences. Not that we hated each other, but we simply were two different people and did not have much in common. Besides, I am introverted, so I would have just kept to myself in any case. Also, he was dating my sister, which is as good enough a reason to dislike someone, right?

Despite these facts and the insistence of my coworkers that I am emotionless and quite possibly a robot, I was an emotional wreck during these events. I struggled for some time, wondering how I could be so attached to someone I hardly knew, and the answer would eventually find its way to me. It was his heart.

Your heart is unable to lie to itself. It feels whatever it wants to feel, and there is little you can do to trick it into thinking otherwise. It is also fragmented into thousands of figurative pieces. Every time we meet someone of any significance to us, we exchange pieces with each other. We do not choose how big or small the pieces we take and give are, but these pieces can shrink or grow over time. Although Chris and I had initially exchanged small fragments of our hearts when we met, his pieces would unknowingly to me, grow larger than I would have expected. It grew from the relationship he had with my family. It grew when I saw the respect he gave to my sister. It grew when I saw his love for their daughter. Therefore, when he died, my heart could not lie to itself. It could not reject what was there even if it desperately wanted to at the time, and that is what heartache is.

The next Monday morning, a week after Chris's death, I eventually came to terms with his departure. I was going through Facebook on my phone, not ready to leave the comfort of my bed. There was one status from my friend Melissa Willard that caught my eye, "I'm just in a complete state of shock right now." The status could have meant a lot of different things, but with the thought of death still fresh in my mind, my instincts pointed in one direction. It was especially alarming because Melissa and I have several mutual friends. I scrolled further down my newsfeed, and there it was. A friend of mine, Carl Yancey, had just died in a hit-and-run accident while he was crossing the street. There was that word again. "What!?"

There are so many good things I can say about Carl. It was not too long ago that he had graduated with a major in sociology. He had already done a lot of social work for the community and was probably planning to use his degree to do even more. He had a way of turning any negative situation into a positive one. He could make you laugh at a moment when you thought there was no way you could. If I went ahead describing every single good thing about him, I could easily fill another ten pages. We got along very well and although we had not spent nearly as much time as I would have liked, we had set up several future projects. We had made plans for podcasts, web series, and we had even thought about doing stand-up together at one point. Unfortunately, none of these projects would come to fruition.

At the time, I was a supervisor in a cash logistics company. Basically, this meant that since money is so essential in our society, nothing could wait. I had to stay until each day's work was complete. I worked through most holidays. I even had to drive through blizzards and hurricanes because it was very important to ensure that banks, ATMs, and stores had their precious money — even while the state had declared emergency conditions. On average, I worked 60 to 70 hours a week, excluding the hour for commuting both ways. As such, any weekend I had an off-duty was, usually, spent relaxing in bed. Normally, I would put everything and everyone off until the "next weekend." It was common for me to blow off family barbeques or my friends for R&R. I justified my anti-socialism with the fact that I was working so much to save up for college and that there would always be time later, but as you can see sometimes, there is no time later.

After Carl's death, I once again became pensive. I wondered why it had to be Chris and why it had to be Carl. Why were they taken at such young ages? I remember specifically thinking to myself, "Carl was crossing a well-lit, empty four-lane street at 9:30 at night in Brockton. He was 6'8" 230 pounds. How could this happen, and of all the scum living in Brockton, why did it have to be the nicest person living there? Why wasn't Chris allowed to see his daughter grow up? Why couldn't he live long enough to marry my sister?"

My only answer was that this was life. Life seldom works the way you would think or want. There are only two things I know for sure about life. First, everyone dies, and second, life is completely random and will do whatever it pleases. It can be tranquil at some points, but it can also abruptly change just as much as every part in this book does. Still, you can always take all the randomness and funnel it down into an idea(s), and put it to good use.

I regret not getting to know Chris as much as I should have. I regret not attending some of his parties. I regret not having recorded anything with Carl and spending more time with him as well. I am too pessimistic to say, "No regrets! Live life to its fullest! Seize the day..." so I will have to live with my regrets. I do not think it is bad to have them; it is ok to feel sad about a missed opportunity or mistake, especially if it helps you avoid them in the future. It is bad to indulge in regrets or let them block your way through life. What my regrets have taught me is that I need to find more balance in my life.

I was listening to the third episode of *Hello Internet*, and the hosts were talking about the "Four Light Bulb Theory" (You might have heard it called The Four Burners Theory). Essentially, this theory reasons that you have four light bulbs representing a different aspect of your life. Friends, family, work, and health. You have enough energy to light them all equally, but none of them will shine its brightest unless you dim one or all of the others. The hosts did mention that they did feel like there is a bit of a flaw in the analogy in that it doesn't cover loss. Yeah, you can dim a light bulb, but it never mentions what happens when you dim it so much you start to lose friends, or family, or your health starts to decline. There is no sense of equity. I've read online about the theory, and everyone has different thoughts on it and different ways to hack the efficiency of the light bulbs. Maybe you can combine light bulbs sometimes — like by working out with your friends and family or buying another light bulb (paying for someone to make you healthy meals, etc.).

You can talk about the semantics of the theory, but in short, the message is that life is all about tradeoffs. You're going to have to give up things sometimes. Work and school are both important parts of your life, and it would be foolish for me to say otherwise, but your friends and family are just as important. Not every one of my weekends had to be filled with sleep. In the past, I could have found a more manageable job or I could have become better at saying, "No" to my managers. I had heard all the clichés, "It can come at any time," "live for today," and all the others concerning this subject matter, but it all was stored in a box inside my head where I had not given it much attention. And on the other side of the coin, I didn't have to spend every waking moment with my family and friends. That's what balance is all about. Nonetheless, some things do not come together in your mind until they are real. It is always different when things are real, which is why it is important for you to not fall into the same trap I fell.

I'm not one to tell someone how to live their life, because who the hell am I to be able to think I have that answer? Maybe, you want to be a person who is focused on work all the time or health or family. As someone who reads a lot about existentialism and absurdism, I don't believe I can tell you how to live your life. However, if you asked me how I want to live mine, I would say that I want a lot more balance in my life. Maybe there'll be times where I focus a little more on one light bulb then another, but now I have the insight to know that I should return to balance eventually. I was fortunate to learn at, a very young age, what kind of a person I wanted to be. Chris and Carl's deaths showed me that I have to do more, in order to honor and remember them properly, and that I still need to work on the person I want to be. Because I have a large fragment of their hearts with me, they can live on through me, and so I know the task before me. They have shown me that I can be a better person than I had previously set out to be. They have shown me that there is a line to draw between my work and my life. In this regard, I have decided to draw it a lot closer to my feet than I had before.

# Resignation

I recently quit a retail job. Hopefully, it's the last retail job I'll ever have to do. The following is the actual letter that I handed in to HR. Feel free to take inspiration from it when you quit your own job.

Good morning,

It is with my deepest sorrow that I am giving you my two-week notice, as I will be resigning from [company]. The last day I'll report to work is June 22, 2019. While I may miss the customer's complaints about warm bananas, avocados that are either too hard or too soft, and low quantity of baby bok choy, I will be moving into the more lucrative business of ~~embezzlement~~

accounting. I'm sure [company] will miss my hard work and resourcefulness, but I'm sure any number of trained monkeys or orangutans should be adequate enough to fill my position. Please be warned that while monkeys will work for less money and require less maintenance than orangutans, they can be more aggressive. I've learned this ~~while training them myself to create minions for my quest for world domination~~ watching several nature documentaries.

I must say that I am going to sorely miss all of you ~~because I should probably say at least one nice thing~~ ~~because I think most of you are ok~~ because you're all such wonderful people, I guess. I've been working here for almost four years, which is longer than I expected, because of the wonderful teams I've been able to work with~~, but mostly due to my large and growing credit card debt~~. I wish everyone at [company] the best and all the happiness in the world as I go off and ~~fulfil my dream of world domination~~ learn new skills and grow as a person.

Best Wishes,
51

Matt Square

"Peace out dudes. It's been real." — William Henry "President for 30 Days" Harrison (Probably)

PS: Despite the total lack of any serious tone in this letter, I want to assure you that I am ACTUALLY resigning and WILL NOT show up after the 22nd.

# An Absurd Task for a Sisyphus-like Life (Outro)

We did it! This is the last essay of this book. I'd say, "They said we couldn't do it," but no one would have been that invested in this process to actually say anything about this book — at least not for another hundred years when this will be the gold standard of books.

There you have it. Three big pressure points of work: customers, management, and coworkers. Essentially, it's people. We are all really the worst. There is a reason aliens won't visit us; we are all just too intolerable for aliens to travel hundreds of lightyears away to meet a planet of dickheads. What is there to do with this information though? Nothing. We're doomed to live with these miserable people for the rest of our lives. These problems have existed since the birth of retail. I can tell you why I think these problems exists.

The main problem with customers is that they sometime lack the ability to see retail workers with any kind of dignity. Most of the people I know want nothing to do with working in retail, but it's the largest employment sector we have right now. It would be similar to how industry and manufacturing used to be the main jobs in the past, but the difference is you could get those jobs with a high school diploma, and you were paid enough to buy a house.

Somehow, that mentality never switched over when those jobs were replaced by retail. Suddenly, those employed by the main source of work shouldn't have to be paid enough to live off of and can't even rise into management in some stores without a college degree. It's really interesting watching baby boomers continually complain about my store being out of stock of something as trivial as broccoli when they came on a weekend at 8pm. These are probably the same people who say that millennials are entitled.

55

My advice to customers is to just be nice. Not just to retail workers — just be nice in general. If you're being a dickhead and ask me for something in the back, I can tell you right now, it's out of stock whether it's there or not. If you're nice, though, I'll go through every shelf in the back to see if we have the product for you.

Also, don't put refrigerated items in the frozen section. Even if it is a food like chicken that can be frozen we can't sell it anymore. You're just wasting food and other people's time. If you're doing it to spite someone, just know it's never the intended person who has to do the work. Often, I hear stories about someone who has to pay a fine so they pay in all pennies to stick it to the man. Or maybe they'll send junk mail envelopes back with rocks so the company has to pay for postage. These tasks aren't going to the CEO of the company. It barely effects the costs to the company. The person it most effects is the person at the bottom of the chain that now has to do a bunch of extra work because you wanted to prove something to someone, but in reality, didn't. So just be nice.

The next problem is management. The bigger the company, the bigger the problem becomes. This is often because corporate can really only rely on numbers to paint a picture of how stores are doing, and it's up to lower management to tell them what is really going on. The problem is that no manager wants to tell corporate when there is a problem. This leads to cutting corners, telling people to work harder and for longer, cutting costs that are necessary to run efficiently and so on.

I like to use overtime as an example of bad management. A lot of managers will try to mitigate overtime because you obviously spend more money doing so. So, a manager might pressure you to do more work in less time, or throw a bunch of people at one project to get it done more quickly, or cancel other work that needs to be done to prioritize other things.

Overtime is a good indicator of overall workload. When a manager finds that it is becoming a regular occurrence, he or she should really be asking some important questions. Is this team actually big enough to handle the workload? Do they have the tools to do the job efficiently? Is there overtime because resources aren't being utilized well, or is the company not setting realistic goals? A manager could bring up any of these issues to corporate, but who wants to admit there is a problem when he can just cover it up and try to make himself look good?

Another issue is that sometimes managers are just not meant to be a manager. There is a huge need for them, but there will never be enough to fill them all with qualified people. Sometimes, it ends up being the person who works hardest, or the person that has been there the longest, the person with the most knowledge, and, in the worst cases, it is just a person that other management likes. I know this personally because I was a supervisor once. I got the position based off my work ethic, but I had trouble with confrontation, I didn't really care enough about the job, and I can be petty and passive-aggressive, all of which can outweigh my hard work. Just ask Wachner and Rory (sorry for being a bad supervisor, but at least I wasn't Slobodan).

Finally, we've come to coworkers. As I mentioned before, your coworkers can make the job way more tolerable. Then there are the ones that drag you down, don't pull their weight, and/or are socially awkward.

I want to take the time to tell you right now that YOUR WORK IS NOT YOUR FAMILY! It's great if you like your company and you've created a bond with some of your coworkers, but corporations will use that against you if they can. Remember that you can be laid off at any time if the company needs to — aka "Be loyal to us, even though we don't have to show that same loyalty." They'll use it to push you past your normal boundaries, so just remember to take things in context and think about yourself before you do something for a company you aren't comfortable with.

So, there it is. Seems pretty glum, eh? Yes, but that doesn't mean you can't still find enjoyment. In his essay "The Myth of Sisyphus," Camus talks about the absurdity of life. In short, he mentions Sisyphus, who is doomed to roll a rock up a hill for eternity as punishment. Camus asserts that he imagines Sisyphus being happy though, and that we should do the same. Despite the futility and absurdity of life, we should strive to find the beauty in it and laugh in the face of the absurd.

That's my suggestion to you. Find whatever thing makes you happy, whether it's big or small. Maybe it is the bond between your coworkers — maybe it's knowing when to tell your manager to go to hell. It's just retail and not worth taking seriously anyway. Whatever it is, find it and laugh defiantly at the stupid rock you're pushing up a hill.

One more thing... this entire book was written with a Ouija board.
OoOoOOooOOooOooohhhhhhh!

# Ten Items or Fewer or Less

This section of the book is all the little pieces that fell through the cracks of my essays. I took my shopping basket and plucked the freshest haikus, stories, and conversations that didn't have a place in the main menu of essays but make for a wonderful dessert at the end. This is a horribly stupid metaphor, but if you've made it this far into the book, how much can you really care about quality?

## -How I Quit My Job-

I had just finished a call with a potential employer informing me that they wanted to hire me. I left the break room of my current job and, by chance, the Executive Team Lead of HR was at the other end of the hall coming towards me.

We stared into each other's eyes as we drew closer and closer to each other, and just as we passed each other I looked towards floor.

**Julia:** Oh, I thought we were having a staring contest. I totally won.

*Me:* Meh, it doesn't matter, Friday is my last day anyway.

**Julia:** ...what?

*Me:* Friday is my last day of work.

**Julia;** What does that mean?

**Me**: I'm not doing anything after Friday for quitting purposes.

**Julia:** Wait.... What are you saying? I don't understand.

**Me:** You know how some people come in to work and do work? Friday is the last day I'll be doing that here.

**Julia:** So you're giving you're... not two weeks... is what you're saying?

*Me:* Yeah, I guess that is what I was trying to convey.

*-How I Quit My Job Part II-*

When I quit the job from the previous entry, I wanted to do something fun — something memorable, something that would prevent me from ever working at the company ever again mostly. There was one team leader that no one in the store really liked. He liked talking about himself, particularly his muscles, quite a bit. His hair was always meticulously taken care of and there'd be hell to pay if anyone touched it. He lacked a lot of social skills and was quite abrasive.

He didn't like me much, but it was nothing personal; he didn't like anyone really. It didn't help matters that I'm usually passive-aggressive with that kind of behavior. I can remember a time where I had emptied an aisle as I was working on a planogram, and he walked by and asked, "Are you putting up this planogram or taking it down?"

He didn't really need to know, but he liked people to know he was an authority figure, and so I responded, "*That's* a question!" in a sardonically cheerful tone. To be clear, I didn't say that it was a good question, just declared that what he asked was a question and no other information.

He walked away in a huff, mad for no reason, and muttered, "Whatever, no one in this store can answer a damn question." Petty little passive-aggressive things like that can help make the job more tolerable. Everyone has little things that annoys them — in this case, it's my "lack of respect". It made no difference to me that he asked the question; if he really pressed me for an answer, I would have eventually told him, especially if he asked nicely, but of course he's always been a dickhead to me, so I said something that I knew was trivial and would piss him off.

On my last day, I wanted to make sure he knew how I felt about him. I went to the aisle with the douches and grabbed as many as I could off the shelf. I dumped them all on his desk with a sign that said, "I just wanted to let you know how big a douche you are. I couldn't find enough." for him to find when he came in the next day.

Unfortunately, another team lead found out before then and removed it all. Luckily, word gets around quick; he wasn't too happy.

## -Farm Fresh-

I was stocking the breakfast aisle when a woman asked for pancakes. The specific ones she was looking for happened to be on the bottom of my cart underneath a million boxes of other products, and the shelf was empty. I told her we had a second location of the product on an endcap and she looked at the box on my cart and said, "I would like a fresh box." As I dug out the box, I really wanted to say to her, "I understand. After all, it is prime pancake season, and you always want to get the ones that are freshly harvested. Not only do they taste better, but you can get a two-year head start on the expiration date."

## -Nintendo Wii-

I was working one year at a department store when a man came up to the register at the electronics department and asked me for a Nintendo Wii. I grabbed one for him and started to ring him up. While I was scanning the product, the man asked if I knew Jeff, a friend of mine who also worked at the store. I said, "Yes," and the man said he was Jeff's father and asked if he could use his discount. I had said he could, but I would need his employee number to enter it, but unfortunately he didn't know it. I told him if he brings the receipt in they can refund the money at a later date, and he nodded and went on his way.

A couple days later, I ran into Jeff and asked him if he ever helped his dad get the discount. Jeff looked confused and asked what I was talking about. After I explained, his only response was, "Well, I guess I know what I am getting for Christmas."

-Through the Front Door-

One of the stores I've worked at had assigned each department to clean the break room on a specific day of the week after the store closes. Saturday was my department's day to clean up, and a coworker from my department and I started to take care of the trash. One Saturday, we didn't have any trash bags in the break room, so he left to grab another roll of bags while I started sweeping. Ten minutes had passed, and I wondered where he was. I went to the supply closet and found no trace of him, so I wandered around, eventually making my way to the front of the store.

That's where I found him, staring at the front door and for good reason. I looked over at the door and found that there was the front half of a car peeking through the entrance of the store. At 11p.m., someone drove through a bollard, the security gate, and through both sets of the store's front doors. I thought to myself, "I understand the excitement for tax-free weekend, but he kind of missed the mark if he was trying to park in an actual parking spot.

The driver of the car assured us he wasn't drunk, but we had our reservations, due to the slurring of speech, the stumbling about, and the aroma of alcohol permeating his breath. He also assured us that there was no need to call the police. He worked for the bank, and he was, "going there right now to take some cash to pay for all this." Thank goodness. That gave me some reassurance that any employee of a bank could go there in the middle of the night and take some cash if necessary.

The manager decided, despite the driver's best intentions, that we should probably still call the cops, and at this point, the driver made sure to explain he wasn't driving. He pointed to a person in the car and blamed them, despite the driver seat being empty and the accused being in the passenger seat.

That's about all I know. I went back to cleaning and didn't hear anything else about what happened to the driver, but I hope he is doing well and that he still has his job at the bank.

## -Shoulder to the Wheel-

I was having lunch right outside the building with a few coworkers when we noticed a suspicious car in a parking lot across the street. Two men were in the car, and it was facing our building, which was concerning because it is a cash vault. It wasn't much of a secret either — the building was surrounded by armored cars, so it was pretty obvious.

They had noticed that were looking in their direction and started driving around the parking lot for a few minutes before parking, again facing the building. Worried, the manager contacted the police. About 5 minutes later, a parade of police cars surrounded the suspicious car.

It was overall pretty exciting, especially for the father and son in the car. Apparently, the son had just gotten his learner's permit, and his father was teaching him to drive in that parking lot. It was all just a coincidence, but that should teach him to ever drive again.

## -Pizza Time (My Toe! My Toe!)-

There was a pizza place nearby that had a deal that was buy one large pizza and get another half off. My friend Alex and I would take turns buying the pizza, and we'd each have a full pizza to ourselves. The only problem was that we usually forgot who paid the last time we went, until I decided we should keep track using my cellphone. This is what happened the first time we tried it:

**Alex:** Whose turn is it to pay?
**Me:** My phone just says Alex.
**Alex:** So, does that mean it's my turn to pay now or that I paid last time.
**Me:** So I think I figured out a flaw in my plan.

## -Customer Satisfaction-

One of the team leads at a store I was working at was interviewing people to fill positions for the holiday season. I saw her walk into an interview and walk out about two

71

minutes later. I asked her why the interview was so short — it's usually a half hour. She told me that she asked the interviewee, "Tell me about a time you left a customer satisfied," to which he responded, "Do you mean sexually?" She decided she had asked enough questions. He didn't get the job as far as I know.

## -Extreme Couponing-

A customer came into our store once and bought a carriage full of items. Upon getting to her car, she noticed that she had a coupon that she forgot to redeem during her purchase. She packs her car and heads back in towards customer to get the dollar that the coupon afforded her. The real issue here was that she left her car running idle in front of the store while getting her dollar. It was predictably gone when she left the store.

Luckily, the police found the car only a few miles away, engine still running. All the things she bought were still in the car, but her purse was gone. All for a dollar of savings.

## -Mother's Day-

For a short period of time, my store was giving out gift cards to a flower delivery service with any purchase. It was a little weird because it was an electronics store, and customers would often say, "What am I going to do with this?" This promotion was happening in May, so I began telling people to buy their mothers' flowers for Mother's Day. That is, until I said it to an 85-year-old woman who just kind of looked at me weird when I said it.

## -Gluten Free-

While I was working in frozen foods one day, a lady approached me and asked where the gluten-free strawberries were. I told her that we didn't stock any frozen fruit that was specially labelled as gluten free. You know... because there isn't gluten in them naturally. It would be like asking for AA batteries that are Y2K-compliant — you don't need to — they just are.

She assured me that they did exist, and "I bought them here before." Note to customers: if you tell an employee that you bought something before, it generally doesn't help the employee in any way. Especially, if you can't tell us the brand, what the package looks like, what the product even is, if you are describing it oddly, or if you are confusing us with a different store.

At the time, I had worked in the department for just under two years and had filled that section many times, but I couldn't think of anything close to what she was talking about. It got to the point where I was starting to second-guess what I thought gluten was. I don't think she ever found what she was looking for.

### -Hurtful Wrists-

**Me:** Hey, Rob. Mike just said to me, "What did I do? My wrist hurts like crazy." And there was some silence after that and I told him that seemed like a set up for a masturbation joke, but I was too classy for it.

(Later that day)

**Rob:** So, has was your weekend?
**Me:** Weekend-like. Yours?
**Rob:** It was pretty cool. I went sledding.
**Me:** Did your wrist hurt?
**Rob:** No... that was my butt.

### -American Made-

**Customer in the bread aisle**: Do you have any like... American bread?
**Me:** What do you mean? That's kind of a vague question. Are you saying you want something super specific or you just don't want Canadian White?

### -M or N-

One of my jobs had a long counter for me and another supervisor to use as a desk. Nobody liked the supervisor sitting next to me, who I will refer to as Slobodan, and the next couple of stories will revolve around him. He was an idiot,

75

but behaved as if he was knowledgeable and held himself in high regard. He didn't like taking responsibility for anything that went wrong, but he caused a lot of problems. I'm not sure I should say that he had no social skills, but rather he didn't care enough about people to have social skills. It's pretty obvious why he wasn't liked much.

Sometimes, we would play pranks on him to pass the time and be passive-aggressive. When he wasn't around, I took his keyboard and switched the "M" and "N" keys with each other. They're right next to each other, and it's fairly easy to miss that they have been swapped. It took about an hour for him to figure out something was wrong.

He turned and showed me the keyboard and the computer monitor — how the keys were working backwards. I mentioned that it seems weird and that might be due to his keyboard being wireless, and the connection was messing up his keystrokes. I showed him my keyboard and started pressing rapidly between my "M" and "N" keys and said, "See? Everything is fine on mine, and it's a wired keyboard." I should mention that I was typing too fast for him to really see if it was typing backwards or not. I should also mention that I also changed the "M" and "N" keys on my keyboard to match his. I changed them back a little while later, and the other workers and I had our laughs.

### -Slobodan is an Idiot-

Slobodan was really good at bringing down the mood of a room. He often entered and gleefully gave the team bad news or added to our already long list of tasks and walked out with a shit-eating grin.

The job required moving around large amounts of cash, so we had a lot of 8-foot cages to help with that. The shelves and the top of the cage could lift up so that the whole cage could close in on itself to save space when it was empty. On top of one of the cages, I wrote "Slobodan is an idiot." The cage was too tall for anyone to see what I wrote, but if I lifted the top, everyone could see it clearly. When Slobodan left the room after doing something annoying, I would lift the top, and everyone would laugh at him.

One day Slobodan and I were looking at security footage to review a particular mistake another employee made. The cage I wrote on was directly under one of the cameras, and he noticed, even though I was switching through the cameras quickly. He asked what the writing was on top of the cage, and I said, "It says you're an idiot," and he remarked, "You wrote that didn't you?"

I responded, "Obviously, you idiot." He didn't have anything to say after that and just gave an annoying sigh as I kept reviewing the cameras.

## -A Controlled Landing-

Slobodan was taking his first vacation and was flying to another state. I had to take over some of his duties.

**Slobodan**: My plane will be landing by noon on Monday, so if you have any questions you can text me.

**Me**: That's kind of presumptuous of you to say.

**Slobodan**: That you'll need to text me?

**Me**: No, that your plane will land. What if it crashes?

**Slobodan**: Gee, thanks a lot, Matt.

**Me**: Oh, sorry. I guess you're right. Technically, the plane would have landed if it crashed, just not a controlled landing.

*-Chronicles-*

Slobodan wasn't the only person that was a dickhead at the job. I can't remember his name, so I'll just refer to him as Jack. Jack would often berate the other employees for playing video games and explain that getting drunk was cooler and a better use of people's time. We usually just actively tried to avoid him, but he would always try to have conversations with us. If we weren't talking about a topic he was familiar with, he'd butt in and try to change the subject to something else. I was usually pretty good at shutting those conversations down by turning the conversation into nonsense. For example, we were talking about video games and Jack randomly started talking about Vin Diesel.

**Me**: Who is Vin Diesel?

**Jack**: Are you kidding me? Vin Diesel! *Fast and the Furious*!

**Me**: What else was he in?

**Jack**: That, uh, sci-fi movie.... Chronicles...

**Me**: Ohhhhhh yeah! Chronicles of Narnia. I know him now.

**Jack**: No... that's not the one.

**Me**: Yeah it is. He was the lion. Remember? "Yo kids, we gotta dive into that wardrobe and beat that witch!

There was also a time when he tried to interrupt another conversation we were having to talk about the death of James Gandolfini.

**Jack**: Hey, did you guys hear that guy died? James Gando...

80

**Me**: Yeah, yeah, yeah. We all know. Gandalf the grey died, but he came back as Gandalf the White. We all know — get with the times man.

Just a quick note, Jack was eventually fired from the job for getting punched in the face. That's not a typo.

### -The King of Lions-

Randomly, during lunch, I said, "Hakuna Matata" to my coworkers. Doug inquired about the phrase's origin, and Rob and I were in disbelief. We kept the origin a secret to him, but he eventually figured it out. He claimed to have heard it and had just forgotten, but we knew he was lying, and he eventually admitted to never seeing *The Lion King*, and we brought it up whenever we could.

**Me**: This is like that time you lied about watching *The Lion King* isn't it?
**Rob**: If they made the movie about Doug, it'd be called *The King of Lying*.

81

**Doug:** Why wouldn't they just call it *The Lying King?*

## -Where's the ~~Beef~~ Bread?-

**Customer**: Hey, where's the bread?

**Me:** (a frozen foods employee working in the frozen foods aisle): It's right here (points to the door beside me).

**Customer**: No, no, no, I want fresh bread.

**Me**: Oh, that's in the next aisle over.

**Customer**: The aisle marker says it's in this aisle.

**Me**: Yes. Frozen bread.... because we are in the frozen aisle...

**Customer**: Whatever.

## -Pregnant Pause-

I had a manager that was sleeping with an employee who worked in the back room. I didn't really have a problem with it or really cared whatsoever, but apparently, the guy from the back room had a girlfriend and a kid, and the girlfriend cared. Especially when he got the manager pregnant. I didn't know how upset she was until she came in and started punching my pregnant manager. It was an interesting day.

### -Another Management Story-

The cash vault I was working at had a manager that knew he was going to get fired. He was the head manager for the entire building, and by the end of his tenure, he just kind of hung around waiting to be fired. Since he was at the top of the chain for our building, he would have to be fired by the district manager, who lived in a different state. The day came, and the district manager flew into town and fired our manager. I want to remind you that this is a cash vault manager and that he always carries a gun. The district manager, also knowing this, fired the manager and told him to drive him back to the airport as his last duty. Nothing happened, but I just think that I wouldn't ask the guy I just fired to be driving me around with a gun. I also wouldn't have driven the district manager anywhere either if I had just been fired as well. I really don't know what is wrong with those guys, but then again maybe that's why I'm not a manager.

## -Pray for Mojo-

**Coworker**: What do you believe in, Matt?

**Matt**: What are you talking about?

**Coworker**: Like religion. Do you believe in God?

**Matt**: Uhhhhhhh. I guess I don't really believe in anything. I'm just like a cloud that goes wherever the wind takes me. That's all I have for a belief system.

**Coworker**: No, you have to have some kind of religion and believe in some kind of God.

**Me**: Yeah.... Clouds and stuff...

**Coworker**: That's really sad, Matt. You know what? When I go home tonight, I'm going to pray for you. I'm going to pray that you find religion.

**Me**: Uhhhhhhhhhhhhhhhhhhhh, please don't.

## -Research-

**Douglas:** Yeah I heard they had captured Ted Bundy before the murders, but he escaped when he asked to go to a library to do research.

**Rob:** What the hell was he researching?

**Me:** He probably had a book report due.

**Douglas:** He was researching for his case.

**Me:** Or he probably had a book report due...

*-Holiday Spirit-*

**Coworker**: Hey Matt, can I get a ride home?

**Me**: No, it's Thanksgiving, not Christmas.

**Coworker**: But I'd be very thankful if you did.

**Me**: Go to hell.

(One Month Later)

**Coworker**: Can I get a ride home, Matt?

**Me**: No.

**Coworker #2**: Damn, you won't give him a ride on either holiday.

(Just a note, I did give him rides more times than not.)

## -Steroids-

**Me:** You're taking steroids, aren't you?

**Rob:** No... can you really tell?

**Me:** Well, you have been emitting a lot of rage lately.

**Douglas:** And your muscles are abnormally large.

**Me:** And when I saw your balls the other day, they did look strange.

**Douglas:** Yeah, they had look like they shrunk when they were on my chin.

## -Plot Twist-

**Douglas**: (Reading ingredients off a random can in the store.) See? I can't even pronounce some of these ingredients — I feel like they are bad for you. What the hell is vanillin?

**Me**: It's the evil twin villain brother of vanilla. You can tell because of the mustache.

## -The Price Isn't Right-

**Customer**: Hey, what's the price of this camera?

**Me**: $299.99.

**Customer**: No, what's the real price?

**Me**: (Points at the price tag.) $299.99.

**Customer**: Yeah, that's the listed price. What's the actual price you're going to lower it to for me?

**Me**: I can't discount it for you — it's $299.99.

**Customer**: In my country, we haggle the price on everything.

**Me**: That is interesting, but we don't do that at this store, and I don't have the power to change the price.

**Customer**: I come to this store all the time, and I am friends with the store manager. He always gives me a discount on everything.

**Me**: That's great. SHE can do that, but I can't.

(Just a note — he didn't get a discount.)

### -The Man Who Never Aged-

**Rory**: Dick Clark died yesterday. Do you know who that is, Wachner?

**Me**: He's the man who never aged.

**Rory**: Yeah he's the man that never aged.

**Wachner**: He's the man that never died?

**Rory**: Yeah... also the man that never aged.

**Me**: No, I think guys are talking about Dorian Gray again...

(No response.)

### -Kung-Fu Fighting-

I was stocking shelves when the song "Kung Fu Fighting" came on the store's speakers. I could hear a woman behind me singing the lyrics. Just as she finished singing, "Everybody was kung fu fighting, Da-na-na-na-na na na-na na," she turned around and saw me standing there and was completely embarrassed. I guess this would be a good time to mention that I am Asian.

### -Restock Fee-

**Me**: Could you just sign this part of the receipt that acknowledges you know about the 15% restocking fee?

**Customer**: What do you mean restock fee?

**Me**: It's just a fee we charge if you opened the box and return it.

**Customer**: I'm not signing that.

**Me**: I can't give you the camera unless you sign the receipt.

**Customer**: What if it's broken, and I try to return it?

**Me**: We obviously wouldn't charge you in that case. That wouldn't be your fault if that happened.

**Customer**: Yeah, you know that, but what about customer service?

**Me**: Well, it's customer service's job to know the return policy, and they would know it better than me anyway.

**Customer**: But how do I know they know?

**Me**: Well, if you're really worried, when the actual receipt prints out when you purchase it, it will have the return policy on the back of it. Also, the policy is written in very large print next to customer service. You can actually read it right now from where we are standing.

**Customer**: Write, "unless broken" on the receipt.

**Me**: Sure...

*-Latke-*

**Customer**: Can you tell me where the potato pancakes are?

**Me**: Sure thing. (Walks the customer to potato pancake section.)

**Customer**: Is this the only location?

**Me**: Yes.

**Customer**: I bought some here before, but they're a different brand. They don't look like these.

**Me**: I'm pretty sure this is it. I can't imagine where else we would have them.

**Manager**: (Notices me trying to help a customer.) Any questions?

**Customer**: Yeah, I'm looking for potato pancakes.

**Manager**: Yes, this is the only place we have them.

**Customer**: No, you must have them somewhere else. I don't remember being in this section.

**Manager**: ... are you talking about hash browns? (Points down the aisle at hash browns.)

**Customer**: Yes! Those are them.

**Manager**: Yeah, those are hash browns.

**Customer**: Yeah, but they're also called potato pancakes.

**Me**: I don't think so.

**Customer**: (Looks at me and says in an indignant tone.) Yeah, so next time someone asks for potato pancakes, you know what to look for. (Walks away.)

**Me**: (Looks at manager.)

**Manager**: (Shakes head, annoyed at the customer.)

*-A Story from Ruben-*

A customer once asked my friend Ruben to cut her slices of bologna very thin because she was a vegetarian.

*-A Story from Andrea-*

Andrea got yelled at by a coffee shop customer for "making fun of him" by me saying, "No, sorry, we don't," when asked if we take EBT.

*-A Story from Hanna-*

At least once a day, something is 50% off, and I'm asked how much that makes the item. I get people aren't great with percentages all the time, but that's a pretty straightforward amount to figure out.

*-A Story from Kate-*

Some older man, after telling Kate how his grandkids call him Joe and not Grandpa, proceeded to look at her butt and pat her shoulder and say, "My dear, you have a nice bottom." She hasn't worn the pants since then.

*-Do You Work Here-*

I was at a toy store that I didn't work at when a customer approached me and asked for help. She needed help getting a bike down from the top shelf. I told her that I didn't work there. I believe she thought I meant that I didn't work in that department because she asked, "Well, can you find someone that does?" I just responded with a quick, "Sure" and then walked away.

-Wine Parrot-

I was stocking an aisle one day when a woman and her friend came up behind me out of nowhere and said pretty much right in my ear, "How do we buy alcohol here?"

I was spooked, not sensing them behind me at all, so it took me a second to get my bearings and I muttered, "Uhhhhh..." as my brain processed what was happening. They just wanted to know if there was a specific place to pay for alcohol because it was a grocery store. I knew the answer, but all she let me say was, "Uhhhh" for about 2 seconds before she continued walking, saying to herself, "Ugh, you

93

don't know." Her friend, following close behind, echoed, "Yeah, you don't know."

### -Somewhere in the Between-

**Customer**: Do you have any more zucchini? The shelf over there is empty.
**Me**: Oh, did you check up front over there? We have a second section of them, and I think someone just filled that section.
**Customer**: Ugh, I guess I'll just buy them somewhere else.

Later on, I saw her walking around the front past the zucchini. She didn't take any of them. Sometimes, customers want very specific zucchinis from a very particular spot and nothing else will do.

### -The Difference Between an Electrician and a Retail Employee-

**Customer**: Can you tell me how this microphone works?

**Me**: Sure. It takes one AAA battery, and you just attach it to the top of the camera.

**Customer**: How does it work though?

**Me**: It has a 3.5mm headphone jack, and that just plugs into the camera, and it will override the camera's mic.

**Customer**: You don't understand, I'm asking you how the microphone works.

**Me**: You're asking me how microphones work from a technical standpoint?

**Customer**: Yes!

**Me**: I'm not sure...

**Customer**: That's ridiculous. This is your job. My father was an electrician. If you asked him any aspect of being an electrician, he could answer it.

**Me**: Yeah, but he probably had a lot of training, and I'm guessing he didn't work for $8 an hour, so that's not really my problem. I don't think it would change much if I did know how it worked anyway, at least on this low-end consumer-level product.

*-Who Cares Either Way-*

Happy Holidays
If you have strong views on this
It doesn't matter

*-Bells Will Be Ringing-*

It looks like Christmas
All the store's decorations
It's still September

*-Austen Wright-*

Feeling kind of low?
Know Mister Rogers loves you
And all that you are

*-Working in Massachusetts-*

Off to work I go
Through many feet of white snow
Because my job blows

*-Alone-*

You can have great friends
And a loving family
But still feel alone

*-Thesis-*

I hate customers
I really hate management
Don't work in retail

*-Thugonomics-*

He believes in this:
Hustle, Loyalty, Respect
HIS NAME'S JOHN CENA!!!

*-Planning-*

Time to cheer you up
With this haiku I wrote you
Fuck... I've no lines left

*-Here's to Life-*

You do what you do
Then you learn to live with it
And you go forward

*-This Haiku is Seven Episodes Long-*

Building inner strength
So I can beat you with my
Kamehameha

# Podcasts You
# Should Know

Work sucks, I know (she left me roses by the stairs). Therefore, I tend to spend time trying to figure out how to have fun when and where I can. A big part of dealing with office jobs is listening to podcasts if you're able. There's a podcast for everything, so you shouldn't have trouble finding one that suits you. I have a ton that I listen to and that I'd like to share with you.

## Retronauts

Hosts: Jeremy Parish and Bob Mackey
Special Mention: Ray Barnholt, Chris Kohler, Kat
Bailey, Scott Sharkey

A podcast about the history of video games. If there is a topic in gaming you like, they have most likely done one or two episodes on it. Their cut-off seems to be about a decade, so it's not all about Atari, Commodore 64, or an Oscilloscope. Sometimes, episodes will even focus on a recent game and its routes and lineage. Overall very informative and interesting, and the contributors are always very knowledgeable.

## Hello Internet

Hosts: Brady Haran and CGP Grey

Two educational video creators talk about life. The term freebooting came from this podcast, and it also defined the "Two Dudes Talking" genre of podcasting. As a "Two Dudes Talking" suggests, there no specific topic it's just... two dudes talking. There are a few topics that come up often, such as airplane crashes, YouTube issues —both on the user and creator side, — sociology, and flags. I don't know — just listen to it.

## <u>Stop Podcasting Yourself</u>

Hosts: Dave Shumka and Graham Clark

One of the first and most consistent comedy podcasts ever, this is a show with little form or format and mostly tends to be about the idiosyncrasies and details of life and pop culture of the past, present, and future much like those ghosts from that Christmas thing, I guess. You never know what an episode will bring. You might learn what a goblin is, that Abby is her own person, news about Hulk Hogan, who wrote the song "Hey Jealousy," gay dogs, or even about a song about peeling grapes.

## Jordan Jesse Go

Hosts: Jesse Thorn and Jordan Morris

A "Two Dudes Talking" podcast but with a guest! One of the pioneers of podcasting, this show offers over 600 episodes nonsensicalness, vulgarity, and irreverence. It's a very fun podcast, and the hosts always brings the best out of their guests. If you can manage to stomach all of that, then this is the podcast for you, possibly (I've listened to all the episodes and I'm still on the fence about it). So plug it in for external power, be wet as a river, hard as a rock, sleazy like Sunday morning, and other yearly mottos that I can't remember.

## Tights and Fights

Hosts: Hal Lublin, Danielle Radcliff, Lindsey Kelk, and Mike Eagle

Special Mention: Julian Burrell

The most woke podcast about wrestling. If you know how miserable wrestling fans can be (think Comic Book Guy, but for wrestling), this podcast is a safe and welcoming space where you can listen and hear some different views on the "sport." Normally, if you were to go one-on-one with a podcast, you'd have a 50/50 chance of winning. But Tights and Fights is a genetic freak, and it's not normal, so you have a 25% chance at best to beat it. Then you throw Julian Burrell into the mix, and your chances drastically go down. So tap those titles and gronk-a-donk-adoo, cause Tights and Fights is "comin fo" you!

## Retail Nightmares

Hosts: Jessica Delisle and Alicia Tobin
Special Mention: Jay Arner

This one is about the horrors of both working in retail and also of being a customer. It's also about finding out what your favorite grape is and how much money you've spent on the Red Hot Chili Peppers amongst over things. I swear I came up with the idea for this book before I found out about this podcast. These ladies are as lovely as they are hilarious and I would say they are my puppos of my lifetime, but I think it's kind of a weird thing for a guy to declare about two women he's never met.

# The Weekly Planet

Hosts: Mr. Sunday Movies and Nick Mason

Two Australian dickheads talking about red hot comic books, movies, and TV news, which they shoot right up your butthole, or so their theme suggests. The best nerd podcast if you don't care that the hosts aren't always encyclopedic and/or pedantic about the details of comic book heroes no one really cares about. Become a Weekly Wackadadoo because this is clearly is the best podcast ever.

## Just Make the Thing
### Hosts: Claire Tonti and Chanel Lucev

Two lovely Australian ladies giving helpful advice on how to start a thing and see it through until the end. I took a lot of their advice while writing the book and they're part of the reason I managed to finish it. Even if you aren't doing anything creative at the moment, the women are delightful to listen to, and it's worth a listen either way.

# NPR Politics

Contributors: Tamara Keith, Domenico Montanaro, Scott Detrow, Asma Khalid, Danielle Kurtzleben, Mara Liasson, Scott Horsley, Mary Louise Kelly, Ayesha Rascoe, Carrie Johnson, Susan Davis, Phillip Ewing, Tim Mak, Ron Elving, Kelsey Snell, Hansi Lo Wang, Michele Kelemen, Ryan Lucas, Jessica Taylor, Geoff Bennett, Vanessa Romo, Alisa Chang, Sam Sanders, Sarah McCammon, Don Gonyea, Miles Parks, and others

A very well-balanced and informative conversation about politics. I never feel confused when listening, and I find that every contributor is quite thoughtful in their assessments of the news. It has a more laidback feeling to it, which I welcome as a departure from other news programs that I find opinionated or feel only provide very passionate arguments. If you'd like a more standard and daily version of this, I would also recommend PBS Newshour.

## Unladylike

Hosts: Christen Conger and Caroline Ervin

Amazing! A healthy look at feminism from multiple viewpoints. As a straight cis male, this is an enlightening podcast to me. It brings up topics and ideas that I would have never thought of because, as a male, I would have never experienced them. I think a lot of the hate and partisanship we see in the world today is due to people not really understanding each other or looking at things from someone else's perspective, which is easy to do. The hosts will sometimes be called out on their views from a particular episode, and they are great at responding and respecting others' opinions, sometimes even dedicating an episode to it. It just shows that if you really want to be a better person, it is important to be introspective and reflective on oneself.

## Freakonomics

Host: Stephen Dubner

Seems like more of a sociology podcast rather than an economics one, but then again you can argue a lot of economics shapes society and vice versa. For example, incentives shapes people's decisions by how they benefit from them. It's a very accessible podcast, and Stephen is a very good storyteller who can make any subject seem interesting, often asking questions that are otherwise overlooked.

## Planet Money

Contributors: Robert Smith, Stacey Vanek Smith, Jacob Goldstein, Ailsa Chang, Noel King, Kenny Malone, Karen Duffin, Sarah Gonzalez, Cardiff Garcia

Similar to Freakonomics, Planet Money is great at breaking down topics in a coherent and enjoyable format. The main difference is that it is more economic focused and usually about things currently happening in the global market.

## Citations Needed

Hosts: Nima Shirazi and Adam Johnson

A magnified look at how or our news, PR, and media is delivered to us and the real message behind it. Adam and Nima take common headlines and news trends and give them a more nuanced and analytic perspective that is lacking in a world where news is being updated by the second. They often question why a story is written a certain way and ultimately who benefits from it. Definitely an important podcast to subscribe to.

## Intelligence Squared

There is a UK and a US version of this podcast, but the only difference is that they are more likely to talk about their respective regional politics. This podcast showcases live Oxford-style debates about current events with experts from the topic. What is remarkable about the show is that although the opposing side mostly never gets me to change my mind, it often gives me a perspective I hadn't thought of. The debaters are often very good at articulating their point in a way that the even an opposing view starts to make more sense. It is civil discourse at its best.

## Blink-155

Hosts: Josiah Hughes and Sam Sutherland

This is a podcast that dives into the entire discography of Blink-182 and then some. It is an extremely detailed podcast, but those details aren't always necessarily about the band or the song they are discussing. The hosts originally didn't really know each other too well at the beginning of the podcast, so it is also about the journey of two men finding out about themselves and their growing friendship. Sometimes it's about watching TV repair videos on YouTube. What more could you ask for besides maybe actually talking about Blink-182 on a Blink-182-centric podcast that regularly is 2-3 hours long?

## Stuff You Should Know

Hosts: Josh Clark and Chuck Bryant

You probably know about this podcast. It is consistently highly rated everywhere. The gist is they cover and research every topic in the world. It is essentially an encyclopedia in podcast form, but a lot more fun. The hosts have a knack for making even some of the more mundane topics seem a lot more interesting.

# How2Wrestling

Hosts: Jo Graham and Kefin Mahon

New to wrestling? This is a podcast to help you catch up on various wrestlers and the history of wrestling to make the transition into wrestling fandom a little less overwhelming. Even if you've been a die-hard fan for a while, you'll most likely find out new and interesting facts about your favorite wrestler.

## Business Wars

Host: David Brown

Usually released in 6-episode chunks, this podcast consists of Brown explaining the history of company rivalries: Pepsi vs Coke, Adidas vs Puma, McDonald's vs Burger King, and many more. In each series, you'll find out how each company started, what led to the rivalry, the back and forth, and ultimately how the companies got to where they are today (if they even still exist).

## We Got This

Hosts: Mark Gagliardi and Hal Lublin

Subjective choices that are jokingly and objectively looked at until a final decision is made. What is the best trilogy? Hot dogs or hamburgers at a BBQ? What's the best religion? Best 80's sitcom? You'll find all these answers and a couple more on *We Got This*. They don't always answer correctly, but I won't hold it against them (they are some pretty lovable guys).

# Talking Simpsons

Hosts: Bob Mackey and Henry Gilbert

A chronological review of *The Simpsons*. Henry and Bob go into the minutiae of every guest star, joke, reference, plot detail, and behind-the-scenes detail they possibly can. Super comprehensive and funny, this is probably the greatest and closest to an episode encyclopedia we'll get. It's the Encarta of *The Simpsons* and will embiggen your trivia knowledge with its cromulence.

## Mega64

Hosts: Shawn Chatfield, Derrick Acousta, Rocco Botte and Garret Hunter

Special Thanks to Kevin

Anti-Thanks to Eric (The Traitor)

A look behind the curtain of the greatest filmmakers of our generation. The creative forces behind Mega64 talk about their latest videos, current events in their lives, and sometimes video games (if Shawn doesn't cut the podcast short). They also do the skits.

# How Did This Get Made

Hosts: Paul Scheer, June Diane Raphael, and Jason Mantzoukas

A podcast about movies, but not a podcast about how they get made. Every other week, the hosts watch a terrible movie and dissect it. Sometimes, it's a movie that's so bad it's good. Sometimes it's a movie so bad they regret their decision to make this podcast. All times it's magnificent to hear.

## How Did This Get Played

Hosts: Heather Anne Campbell and Nick Wiger

A fairly new podcast with a lot of potential. The same format as *How Did This Get Made*, but instead of movies, they review video games. Also, there aren't many games that are so bad that they are good, so they are basically punishing themselves for our entertainment.

## Cinema Swirl

Hosts: Kefin Mahon and Sam Chaplin

One of these guys has watched a lot of movies. One of these guys has watched very few movies. Together, they revisit classic movies, and the latter of the two learns about the wonder of movies or how powerful nostalgia is and points out how crappy our beloved movies are. They sometimes talk about their soda preferences.

## Nintendo Voice Chat

Contributors: Peer Schneider, Zach Ryan, Brian Altano, Samuel Claiborn, Andrew Goldfarb, Brendan Graeber, Casey DeFreitas, Jose Otero, Richard George, Audrey Drake, Daemon Hatfield, Scott Bromely, Jack DeVries, Craig Harris, Matt Casamassina, Mark Bozon, and Miranda Sanchez

Welcome! Dedicated solely to Nintendo news, this podcast is very informative and very fair in their assessment of the company and its decisions as well as its games. All of the contributors are passionate and knowledgeable about the company and even when delivering bad news, they are good at making the podcast fun.

## This Sounds Serious

Written By: Dave Shumka, Peter Oldring, Pat Kelly,
and Chris Kelly

Special Mention: Carly Pope

A real fake crime podcast. If you're tired
of listening to the recent trend of true crime, this
satire of them might be just the thing you've
been waiting for — maybe. The first season
focuses on the murder of a beloved weatherman
and the reporter that is just trying to find
answers. A truly hilarious podcast worth listening
to.

## Everything's Coming Up Simpsons

Hosts: Allie Goertz and Julia Prescott

A comparatively less comprehensive look at *The Simpsons*. Each week, Allie and Julia talk about the guest's favorite episode and often how it impacted decisions in their current careers. They have been through most of the popular episodes and are currently on hiatus to do interviews and podcasts that touch on people or other media that are tied to the Simpson universe. The two charismatic and inviting hosts do a wonderful job speaking to the spirit of the episodes and don't get too bogged down by the trivial details. I just think they're neat.

## Dr. Death
Host: Laura Beil

Absolutely horrifying. A true story of a surgeon, who despite being unqualified and unfit to perform his job, went from hospital to hospital destroying lives. His malpractice led to two deaths and 33 patients who were seriously injured, many of whom were many left with permanent pain or impairment. The scariest part to me is that how this could have happened to anyone, as we generally put a lot of trust in doctors and hospitals, but somehow this guy got through. It was hard to listen to, but at the same time, I was waiting every week to hear the next episode.

## More or Less

Host: Tim Harford

A podcast that takes an in-depth look into the statistics that pop up in various forms of media. Often, the numbers in the news can be unreliable or misleading. *More or Less* is here to examine claims that are made and double check the sources behind them. It's a short, but enlightening podcast.

## AE Podcast

Hosts: Kefin Mahon, Adam Bibilo, and Billy Keable

Oh, you didn't know? Well your ass better listen to AE Podcast. A full revisit and examination of the Attitude Era of professional wrestling. They go through each pay-per-view during that time frame with both thoughtful and hilarious insight.

## <u>OSW Review</u>

Hosts: Jay Hunter, Steve (Mr. OOC), and Stephen Roe
Special Mention: Maffew

Similar to the AE Podcast, but these guys tend to focus more on the Hogan era of wrestling. They're all Irish, they are all funny, they like *The Simpsons*, and they like video games. So if you know what candy bar you are and like all those other things, this may or may not be the podcast for you.

## All Systems Goku

Hosts: Dan Ryckert and Jeff Gerstmann

Two men who have never watched any anime watch and review all of *Dragonball Z Kai*. It's interesting to hear them try to understand some aspects of anime while realizing that some of their favorite things, like wrestling, are basically a different version of anime or anime inspired. They are finished with the series and are now Anime masters. They do plan to do the other *Dragonball* series in the future, so stay tuned for another exciting episode of *All Systems Goku*!!!

## The Indoor Kids

Hosts: Emily V. Gordon and Kumail Nanjiani

I think this podcast is done. The hosts went on hiatus because they were both getting more opportunities in the year 2015. But, if you are wondering what the now famous Kumail and Emily were thinking about nerd culture between 2015 through 2016, this is the podcast for you.

## Retsutalk

Hosts: Slowbeef and Diabetus

Two guys who talk over Let's Play videos on
YouTube, a la MST3K-style, decided to start a
podcast to talk about that and other random
things. Then, one of them had kids and now they
do neither, but you should still listen to it.

## Takoyaki Time

Hosts: Bry Scalley and Kate Bresnahan

A podcast made by two friends of mine. They talk about anime and Japanese culture. Even if you aren't familiar with an episode's topic, they are all still worth listening to. These ladies are so charming that it is entertaining listening to them talk to each other. It's like being a part of a friendly conversation.

## Two Date Minimum

Hosts: Madelein Smith (That's how you spell her name, don't bother me, I double checked) and Woody Battaglia

I don't know what this podcast is about, and I've never listened to it. But it has my very funny friend and comedian Woody, so it has to be good. I don't know Madelein either, but if Woody is ok with her, she must be perfectly adequate as well. I don't, but you should just listen to it.

# Acknowledgements

I can't end this book without thanking everyone I know for no apparent reason, so...

**Whoever is editing this (WordWiz from EditorWorld.com):** Thank you. Consider yourself as the only person to ever read this book. Also, sorry you had to read this book.

**Argama Witch:** Thanks for making the cover of this book for me. It really brings the whole book together. I would say I would like to collaborate with you again, but writing books is kind of annoying and time-consuming.

**Ruben Pagan:** You were the best of friends, you were the BLURST of friends?! You snore way worse than I do. YOU DIDN'T TELL ME THIS BOOK WAS THREE HOURS!

**Brooke Pagan:** I would like to take the time to thank you and your husband for always being there for me and showing me what true friendship is. It's really too bad I'm moving to California and never seeing either of you ever again.

**Amanda Brown:** Thank you for forgiving me and sticking with me, even though I'm an idiot who doesn't know what feelings are. We've been through a lot, but we learned a lot about ourselves, and we did have a lot of fun times and continue to have them. Don't forget how awesome of a person you are.

**Sizzlack:** I feel like I've only ever met you twice, but both times was very inspirational and dope.

**Alex DaSilva:** You have too many muscles. I would like some. Also a hug.

**Diana:** You are like the lady version of me. Only if I were cooler. Also, if I were a lot more attractive. And if I had a cuter nose. Plus a lot of other things, but we're friends and that's all that matters at the end of the day.

**Jack Soohoo:** It's not worth the stardust to acknowledge you.

**Jenn McCarthy:** Did you know that Brooke used to work at a pizza place? I don't remember which one; she doesn't bring it up much. PS: Did you know that I am one of your favorite people in the world? PPS: Do you remember that band Five?

**Pat McCarthy:** If I have ever taught you anything, I'm glad it was that DDP's theme was basically "Smells Like Teen Spirit."

**Mekenzie Berry:** To my fiancé, all my love for eternity and something about big black dicks.

**Ashley McKenna:** Your breasts look amazing, but nothing will ever compare to you absolutely charming personality and no amount of money can buy that.

**Alex Guaraldi:** STEP!

**Christopher Van:** I can't remember if your name has two n's or one, but in my last book I wrote it with two. That means at least one of these times is correct, assuming it is not somehow three n's.

**Amber:** I really appreciate that you let me play with your cat whenever I come over for game night. He is quite a special cat. You're ok, too.

**Tom Carroll:** Who would have thought that we'd still be friends for this long? I would have thought at least one of us would have died of some kind of asbestos-related illness by now.

**Nick Destefano:** You slept over my house in high school once. We snuck out of the window in the middle of the night to wander the streets of our town. There was no reason why we had to exit through that window. We were in the basement

141

and could have easily left through the basement door without alerting anyone. But leaving through the window made us feel like we were doing something wrong. Something edgy and cool. I imagine that line of thinking would define how we would act in high school and I'd like to think that we have grown out of the phase, but sometimes I really want to leave through the window.

**Nathanial Karahalis:** Here's to the greatest trombone I've ever seen... possibly. Let's start a really bad ska band.

**Billy Reardon:** Congrats on being an accountant. From one accountant to another, I can say we are now basically the same person. Except for all the differences.

**Brian Farrell:** DontTalk2Me about that time you shot lasers out of your eyes.

**Sean Sargent:** Wacky Tacky.

**Bill Cate:** Someday, we'll get together and finish what we started on. Doctor Gristle.

**Eric S:** Bacon Foster.

**Eddie:** Thank you for reading my other book. Not only that, you were so enthusiastic about it. I can't believe you are gone. I wish we could have spent more time together.

**Rob Curtis:** Thanks for all the Mattbert Shorts you were in. Thanks for being a good friend in general. Most of all, thanks for watching me put a bunch of douches on that guy's table.

**Beth Hinkley:** "The years start coming and they don't stop coming. Fed to the rules and I hit the ground running. Didn't make sense not to live for fun. Your brain gets smart, but your head gets dumb." — English proverb

**PJ Saengsombat:** I just wanted to let you know that you're a gangsta, you're a straight-up G.

**Bob Klingerman:** Sometimes you just need to know when to hold 'em.

**Tony Rocca:** Sometimes you need to know when to fold 'em.

**Dave Johansson:** Sometimes you need to know when to walk away and know when to run.

**Collin Henderson:** You can't defeat me. No man can defeat me!

**Dan Foran:** Always remember that the original singer of "Girls Just Want to Have Fun" sounds like Dracula.

**Victoria Tucker:** Thanks for not know that I worked at the store for several months. Hope you don't have to work self checkout anymore.

**Jeromy Carter:** Hustle, loyalty, and respect.

**Wachner Andre:** I just want you to know that Jeromy is a PS. He probably still doesn't have a license that idiot.

**Rory D'Alessandro:** I may be Mattbert, but I'll never be Matty B. I'll do the best I can.

**Tony "Clash" Medina:** You're the only professional wrestler I know personally. That also means you are the best wrestler I know personally. You may not have a championship right now, but you'll always be the champion of my heart.

**Deb Frasca:** You're the best mom I never had, but always wanted. Remember that the punchline to the best joke I ever told you is Dick Van Dyke.

**Ryan Sears:** You're gonna owe me a lot of pretzels.

**Zane Pendergast:** Remember our band Returns to 72? I'll never let you forget for as long as I live.
145

**Rodrigo Hernandez:** BOOM! Out the window.

**Billy Hernandez:** I like ponies.

**Richard Hernandez:** Since you are accustomed to cold temperatures, I'll take all the blankets.

**Michaela Sharpone:** Remember when you quit, and I told that lady that she could go to hell?

**Xavier:** Have fun counting those dips and dressings without my help. They always leave the worst jobs for us minorities. Bastards.

**Brad Whitney:** You and your brother are both giant dickheads. The only difference is that your brother is a professional wrestler that is paid to be a dickhead. I don't know what your problem is. Just kidding — please don't fire me.

**Samm Brush:** Sorry I quit my job and I couldn't follow you from department to department until the end of time. I will still schedule all of my time off based off your time-off requests though.

**Ryan Bastian:** I hope by the time you are reading this that wrestling has gotten much better. It probably hasn't, but I'm always willing to start a wrestling promotion with you as an alternative. Start practicing your moves on various coworkers.

**Brittany Gauvin:** You are currently the best at shelving bread and all the activities that are included with that responsibility. If you're ever angry, just imagine that I'm bringing you candy or just count the months until you'll get my Christmas card.

**Ryan Hickey:** I'm glad we could bond over our love of Avril Lavinge's music. It's what separates us from that kid in the background. Well, that and the whole odor thing. Oh, and the work ethic. Pretty much everything actually...

**Thais Fernandes:** I hope someday you have a job that doesn't require you to fill in shelves of chips or candy by the dairy section. You are the baddest bitch.

**Sarah Meacham:** Since we are no longer able to park next to each other, I sincerely hope that your car is doing well. I hope the bread you make serves you well.

**Mandy Lovell:** If you ever need someone reliable to put a pallet of watermelons in the cooler, you just let me know. I don't know if I can help you with that anymore, but I also think you don't really care about that anymore now that you changed departments. It's the thought that counts, I guess.

**Donna:** I hope by the time you are reading this you have two kittens, and I'll have seen just as many pictures of them that I have shown you of mine. Also, you can imagine while I'm typing this that I am posing like a model.

**Donna (Deli):** Thanks for leaving the deli section for dairy and not telling me. I found you anyway. Nice try!

**Jean:** Why are these bananas so hot? Also, do you have any arugula?

**Nicholas:** I'm leaving and I'm never coming back.

**Bob Newman:** It has been a pleasure filling in the ice endcaps with you over the years. I will never forget all off the frozen training you gave me.

**Lauryn Baker:** You are a very kind a motherly woman and I appreciate all of the warmth you have given me over the years. I also appreciate your ability to drop gold coins everywhere and pick them up as your daughter watches.

**Keanu Allen-Ortiz:** Don't let the bastards grind you down, whether it be at work or politically. Like Howard Dean always says, "Take back the White House, YEAAGH!"

**Lisa (Front End):** I just wanted you to know that you're the bestest and prettiest of the front end ladies that I know. Just don't tell anyone else that I told you that. See you the next time my office sends me to randomly buy a bunch of lottery tickets!

**Stephanie Boyle:** We never went apple-picking like we had planned in 2009, but I'm assuming the offer is still open until the end of time.

**Holly Coots:** I met you once at Stephanie's party, and we haven't seen or talked to each other since, but we're still friends on Facebook, and I think you're cool enough for a run-on sentence in this random book.

**Rose Locatel:** Once, I was measuring something in my head by holding my hands in the air. You turned around as I was doing it and asked if I was motioning for a hug and I was going to respond that I was not. Then, I thought that it would be easier to just hug you than to explain what I was doing, and we've been friends ever since and I don't ever regret it.

**Kate Ciavara:** I probably wouldn't say this to your face ever, but I wanted you to know that I really admire you. Having hung out with you this past year, I learned that you and I eerily have a lot in common when it comes to life issues we are trying to work out. As someone who is trying his best to work things out and move forward in life and be happy, I can say a lot of times I just would rather stay in bed all day long, even if I have something fun planned. I already thought you we cool when I met you, but I realized how amazing you were when you kept staying on all your creative endeavors, going to craft fairs, and staying positive and optimistic through it all (or at least trying to). So, thanks for being awesome! I hope this didn't trigger some kind of anxiety response from you.

**Cara Goulding:** Just letting you know
I like your resting bitch face
Though Michelle does not

**Nicole Ellis:** I, Titus Uno, Certified Public Accountant, Forensic Certified Public Accountant, and Chartered Global Management Accountant, thinks you're pretty great.

**Jacqui Frasca:** I believe in you more than I believe anyone I've ever met. You are destined for greatness, not necessarily in your career, but rather in life. You are strong, resilient, and thoughtful, and I wish you the most radical of times. Just remember to go your own way, Fleetwood Mac style.

**Michelle Frasca:** I was going to write something about our friendship, but we only ever talk for about 10 minutes at a time, once a year. It still feels like I've known you forever, and we know each other well, but that is just one of those things, I guess. Either way, I'll see you at Veggie Galaxy.

**Austen Wright:** To my friend Austen / My life is that much greater / By having known you

**Ryan Coomey:** You mean to say that I wrote about you at this time of year? At this time of day? In this part of the book? Localized entirely within the acknowledgment section? Yes. May you see it? No.

**Bry Scalley:** I hope someday you run for president and can smash the patriarchy. If you do, I suggest we change our national bird and song. I also suggest that we finally have a national anime.

**Justin Tribuna:** You once told me that you had the band The Mountain Goats sign a Mountain Goat Magic™ card for you. That's all I really know about you, but it's quite the fact.

**Kate Bresnahan:** I just wanted to let you know that I'm sorry if I come off as a creep. I *AM* actually a creep, but I try not to be *that* kind of creep. Also, I'm also sorry that statue of a deer fell on top of you that one time.

**Dane Sager:** I still want to have a James Bond cover band with you called "4 Non-Bonds." If nothing else, we should at least write a movie about four turtles who have mutated into teenaged ninjas.

**Ray Ortiz:** I hope someday you find the answers to life that you are looking for. If you don't, we still have time to create that minority-based tag team and travel the world honing our wrestling skills.

**Sarah Dauplaise:** Thank you for reading my last book. You were one in probably 2 people that did. I didn't take my pants off in this one, but I believe the quality of this book is better. Not much better.

**Susan Chong:** Maybe someday I'll come to Seattle and visit you. Probably not, but maybe. Either way, I wish you the best of luck seeing the cutest of animals.

**Andy Carlson:** The last time I saw you, Boston had just beaten Seattle in some kind of sporting event. I hope that doesn't sour you on our friendship or bring up any bad memories.

**Tara Vilk:** We were both Red House Representatives, but I just walked into the club and randomly decided to run for the position and got it. I don't know how you feel about that, but if you have any negative feelings, this book is a written contract between us for one free punch at me.

**Joe Scurio:** We never finished playing "Four Swords Adventures." What's up with that?

**Trevor Cross:** I once arrived and told you that I had just come from the mall and that I had just punched a child in the face. You questioned my motive for this and when everyone asked why you would believe me, you responded, "Because it's Matt, and anything he says — no matter how bizarre — could potentially be true."

**William Lopez:** It's all politics. Whatever you were asking me — that's the answer.

**Woody Battaglia:** I'm sorry that, for a period of time, you had no skin. You did, however, get to see me in a Robin costume on stage, so I do believe in karmic balance as a result.

**Erika Marit Iverson:** Thank you for sitting with me during breakfast at MaxFunCon East. It was great getting to know you, and I'm sure there are to be many fun adventures ahead. Maybe? Possibly...

**Matthew Falls:** I feel as though with each new Zelda game, your mustache becomes more and more majestic. I don't have anything to prove this, but I don't have any evidence to disprove it either.

**Darcie Roy:** I never thought I would meet someone at that store that would like ska as well. But I did, and where has that gotten us? Here's to you, kid (even though you don't like being called kid) and all the planograms we've set and all the friends we made along the way.

**Matthew Bruso:** I don't know whatever happened to you, but I hope it was good.

**Jeannetta:** You were the realest and nicest to me of anyone on the team, which is why you are the only one here. Thanks for being genuinely nice to me and for all the good times.

**Michelle Wentworth:** I am very glad I got to meet you. You are one of the more pleasant people I have met in retail, and that karaoke outing was delightful.

**Melissa McGuiness:** I'm glad we could have a positive impact on each other's lives. You are a super cool person, and that concert we went to will be one of my favorite life events.

**Jen Pendergast:** When your brother and I were in a band together, I wrote a song about not wanting to be in a relationship with someone who didn't have a live dinosaur. There's a reason why we are no longer in that band, but I wouldn't totally blame that song.

**Alex Stavrenos:** Thank you for being one of the first people to be in Mattbert Show. It is nice having a friend that is up for anything. You'll always be one of my best friends, and I'll always be thankful for the music you have imparted me with.

**Caitlin Martinez:** I miss hanging out with you a lot. I miss your cats more, but you were pretty tolerable. You still need to take me snowboarding, too.

**Chris Carty:** We always talk about ideas we have for skits we want to film. We never do them though. We should regress further and talk about ideas of skits we would potentially tell each other... eh, never mind... this is getting too complicated. But it is a good idea to film a skit.

**Garrick Hunt:** Thank you for believing in my photography skills. In return, I will believe in your bass guitar skills. Together, we can believe in each other's inability to create a Technodrome.

**Ashley Smith:** I gave you a birthday gift once and only once. I don't know why, but you got it, and we had lunch together that day. You are also one of the palest people I know.

**Holly Taylor:** Sorry my pictures of your wedding weren't that great. But you should have known that I'm not really good at anything. If you guys ever have a second wedding for some reason, I'll pay for a better photographer.

**Nick Taylor:** I just want you to know that I know that you are a man that exists. I don't know much else about you. Actually, aside from your name and that you exist I literally know nothing about you. Your job, your race, your voice, your face, nothing...

**Shaun Papineau:** You are a very abrasive person. You seem to be okay with that though. At least you are nice to me because I gave you the extra copy of *Ocarina of Time* that I had in my trunk.

**Laura Hunt:** I remember when we first met, I had to change my phone plan because we texted each other so much. I don't know what you're up to now, but I assume you are on to greater things. Most likely building a giant skyscraper sized robot to defend Earth from giant monsters. Also, I'm moving to Australia to hang out with your sister.

**Danielle Brodeur:** I thought we'd be married by now, but you keep getting all these boyfriends. Oh well. At least we'll always have the drive-in and the banana costume.

**Melissa Willard:** I taught you how to develop film, and you taught me how to develop my stylish lab coat. One of things isn't true, but who is to say it won't be true in the future. I mean... it won't be true in the future either, so I guess the answer is me.

**Mr. Martin, Mr. Burley, and a large number of BHS teachers I don't have time to list here:** As teachers in my formative years, this book is a testament of the student you nurtured. You should feel ashamed.

**Jennifer Roche:** Thank you for giving me the confidence to write this book. I owe it all to you, much to the chagrin of everyone else, but I'm glad and that's all that matters.

**Caitlin Golden:** You've been an amazing professor and advisor, but I want to make sure you know I didn't use anything you taught me in accounting in this book. EXCEPT for that it meets all eligible GAAP standards.

**Mark Crowley:** Like I had mention to Caitlin, none of what you taught me as an accountant is in this book. I can, however, tell you what the future value of this book is (it doesn't look to good for me).

**Stephanie Jacobsen:** Thanks for being an awesome professor. I had a radical time in your class, and it really came at a good time to help me get through a rough time.

**Joseph Williams:** I feel that we are destined to run into each other, at conventions, wearing the same costumes for eternity.

**Aubry:** You are one of my favorite persons ever! You are absolutely delightful and I hope someday we can go biking together.

**Matthew Whitlock:** I am surprised that you remembered about Disco Stu and the Neon Salamis. They never took off as well as I would have liked, but I hope when you become a huge musical producer I can count on you to get their name out there.

**Mike Khorshidianzadeh:** You are a man that I highly respect. Whether it is your opinions on politics, philosophy, or comic books, I value your insight. I'm glad you've become a teacher and are hopefully nurturing young adults who will lead us to a prosperous future. Also, if you ever need to shorten your last name, mine could use a couple more letters.

**Laura Viera:** Once we went to Warped Tour together, and you weren't feeling well, but instead of just driving you home, I watched one more band I wanted to see before taking you home. I still think about what a crappy thing that was to do to this day, but now that you are a trained MMA fighter, you're more than welcome to settle things in the octagon.

**Alfred Tripolone:** I don't know why you kicked a hole in that wall or what made you think you could run on one. I will, however, admit it was quite a humorous experience. Also, if the hotel that was involved is reading this book, this is no admission of guilt by any parties. We're not giving you any money!

**Andy Hatchfield:** We stayed in a hotel together because we went to the Warped Tour in Fitchburg. I remember that I had given you a piggyback ride from the parking lot, up a set of stairs, and in 100-degree weather. It's still the most athletic thing I've ever done.

**Stephen Hatchfield:** You may never be Superman, but you'll always be the Superman of my heart and my dick.

**Justine Pickering:** The best manager I have ever had. Your bright and positive demeanor really made the job fun. Thanks for all your help with the job and with life in general. Your car isn't as dirty as you think.

**Jill Bourgault:** Thank you for listening to all my problems at work and for all the shared lunches. I don't know who is getting your Friday coffees now, but if you give back my damn Christmas stuff, I'll get you another coffee.

**Lynda Campbell:** Thanks for all your help and advice and everything and things and stuff. You are a very wonderful and loving person. You're still a brat though, and that's where your daughters get it from. Just kidding (kind of) — you're the best!

**Alyssa and Hannah Campbell:** Your mother is a wonderful woman, so don't be brats. I'm a big enough brat for her to handle alone.

**Shireen:** I'm only putting you in her because you are so sensitive and would be mad if I didn't. You are a pretty horrible person though.

**Kristen Brown:** My birthday is in June, I don't know who told you it is in March. Thanks for not laying me off. It's nice to have a job sometimes. I don't know about this job specifically, but whatever.

**Kristin Filo:** Sorry I'm not as good at sorting mail, but also I don't really care. Yoda said, "Do or do not" and I DO sort the mail. On a similar note, Chewbacca once said, "RAWRGWAWGGR," which is always something that I take to heart and something that you should, too.

**Felicia Dern:** I'm glad to have worked with you and to have hated most of the same people at work. If you ever need flowers for Valentine's Day ever again, you just let me know. And one last thing, Asian people don't use dishwashers, trust me.

**Dawn Higgins:** Thanks for all the advice you've offered me over the years in life and work. You were easily the most fun manager I've ever got to work with. Keep doing those stretches!

**Reginale Dujour:** Thanks for all the movie and TV show recommendations. I'll never watch them, but thanks anyways!

**Talbot Hazard:** Hopefully a war has not started from the time of me writing this to the time it is published, but as you always say, "we're all gonna die." Sorry to remind you of your mortality in my book.

**Joanna DaVeiga:** Thank you for the job opportunity. This is the best job I've ever had. Hopefully, by the time you are reading this we have both completed Federal Taxation, and we never have to think about it again.

**Jovany Melendez:** If you are reading this, I may or may not have lost weight. If I haven't and I'm eating something while you are reading this, knock it out of my hand.

**Jared Grimes:** I would tell you to order this book on Amazon, but I can't guarantee it will ever be delivered to the office.

**Emma Battaglia:** When you are working for the *New York Times*, do you think you can get me onto the bestseller list? Please?

**Georgia and Zeik Savory:** You saw the silly, but creative, student inside me and let that creativity flourish. You gave me the inspiration to write my first book and by proxy, this one, too. I'm thankful to have known both of you!

**Amanda Bernard:** I really enjoyed going to the museum with you. We will have to return soon. I hope that everything in your life comes into alignment, and you can find something really worth living for.

**The Morales Family:** Thank you for letting me into your family. Lots of fun times, pictures, and good food. I love you all and wish for much happiness and Halloween parties for all of you. (At least we don't have to worry about Halloween costumes at work anymore.)

**Hilary Marcelli:** I once took a compatibility test at BHS, and it said that you were one of my top matches. That means in a different world, we could have watched a lot of pop punk concerts together as a couple.

**Jaymie Bowles:** It took us too long to decide to be friends, but we're friends now. You are far more passionate about everything you involve yourself with. I can really admire that, as you are more passionate about any one goal than I am about everything I'm passionate about combined. Don't forget to slow down sometimes and appreciate the little things, too!

And finally, gentle reader, I'd like to thank you. "What's that?" you say? Me thanking you? No, it's not a misprint, for you see, I enjoyed writing this as much as you enjoyed reading it.

# Endut! Hoch Hech!

(What the hell was that?!)